SENSUALLY BEAUTIFUL

EB TAYLOR

Printed by Amazon Inc., in the United States of America.

First printing, 2022

Lyla D Creations LLC
24445 Painter Drive
Land O Lakes, FL 34639

www.lyladcreations.com

Cover by: Carter Cover Designs
Formatted by: Carxander Publishing

Table of Contents

DISCLAIMER

The poems contained in this book are sexually explicit.

Continue to read at your own risk.

DEDICATION

To anyone who fell for the wrong person.

To anyone who was fooled by someone.

To anyone who's love comes from their soul.

To everyone:

Always be kind.

TIED

I feel so

Tied up

With him.

But not how

I wanted

To be.

DESSERT

As I lick my large glass that held the brownie ice

cream dessert,

I think of the time my tongue licked you.

All sweet,

Delicious and sinful

A warm brownie,

Ice cream,

Whipped cream,

Hot fudge,

And you.

BOOTS

I slip on my thigh high boots,

My short leather skirt,

My black silk blouse.

Excited to meet you,

At our secret place.

I lay back and watch you undress.

I watch as you undress me.

You slide each boot from my legs.

Dragging your fingertips

Along my skin.

You stand before me,

A vision I thought I'd only ever dream of.

But today,

You make my dreams come true.

As you crawl onto my naked body,

And fuck me until I reach my bliss.

SOFT

I love your soft skin against mine.

Your hands upon my body,

Your face between my thighs,

Your soft hair tickling me

As your tongue

Licks me

Tastes me

Devours my body.

I love your sweet soft voice

Whispering against my neck

Your soft breath tantalizing me.

Your soft sparkling eyes

Gaze deeply into mine.

We speak in silence.

Our desire is the same.

For all eternity.

OH MY!

Oh my, you are beautiful.

I want you.

Between my lips,

Between my legs.

As long as you're inside me,

Oh my!

My hands bumping down your abs.

As your hard cock thrusts deep into me.

Your hands grip my hips.

Moving my body up and down.

Fucking me brilliantly,

Oh my, baby.

Oh my!

DELICIOUS

You were delicious.

Tender, warm, fierce.

Your skin against mine

Felt like silk.

Meet me again.

I want to taste you,

Touch you again,

Meld into you,

Breathe you in,

Make love to you again,

And again, and again.

You are the most delicious man

I've ever met.

LAST NIGHT

Thank you, baby.

Last night was fabulous.

You were delicious,

Intoxicating, ferocious.

You bested the wildest,

Wettest dreams.

Your hands,

Your mouth,

Your firm body.

Oh my!

Thank you, baby.

You were fucking amazing,

Last night.

THAT ONE TIME

That one time.

My tongue enjoying a trip down your body.

Meeting your perfect ripples,

On my way to your treasure.

Mmm,

How glorious you were.

Inside me,

Both ways.

Delicious,

Powerful.

That one time.

It was worth

Every

Fucking

Thing.

CHAMPAGNE TRICKLE

The champagne trickles down my throat.

Reminds of when you did.

You were so sweet,

So slick,

So yummy.

I miss you, love.

Things have changed.

You can't reach me anymore.

But that memory of you tasting like

A champagne trickle,

Baby, that's forever.

50

So young,

Thin, tall, fit, firm.

Blue eyes, brown hair.

So young,

And friendly.

A beautiful smile,

Perfect white teeth.

So young,

So yummy.

BLISS

She connected with him today.

As she laid on her bed,

Vibrator turned on high.

Thinking of him being there instead.

She suddenly saw him,

Clear as if he laid beside her.

She repeated his name over and over.

Their connection clicked.

He turned and smiled.

Her body quivered catching his gaze.

She screamed his name

As the vibrator brought her to her bliss

She will one day share with him.

TONIGHT

As I drink my whiskey,

I want to rip off your clothes,

Climb your body,

Kiss your sweet lips,

Taste you,

Caress your soft skin.

Tonight

As I sip my whiskey,

My inhibitions disappear.

I want to fuck you all night long.

Awaken next to you,

Embraced by your arms.

Baby, I love you,

Stone sober or not.

HANDCUFFS

You want me in handcuffs

Don't you?

You enjoy the control you have over me.

Silencing me,

Restricting where I can go.

You love controlling me.

Putting me in handcuffs,

That's your fantasy.

Do you want to just watch?

You want to see how I look

Hands restrained,

Unable to stop you.

Not that I would.

Stop you, that is.

I can make this happen

Whenever you want.

LEATHER

The leather seat holds my ass

While our bodies meld.

The coolness of that black leather

Against my body as I lay under you

Won't stop the inferno inside me.

Your sedan is the perfect place

To devour one another.

I can't remove my dress and panties

Quick enough to give you the access you so

desire.

A tug on your pants, and there you are.

Oh baby, how I long for you inside me.

I gaze at you from your leather seat,

Catch your beautiful eyes with mine.

Your grin so full of trouble.

Your firm body full of sin.

We make passionate love

On your soft leather seats.

Forbidden as it is,

Our lust, desires,

Needs for the other

Take control,

Win the night.

KINKY

Everyone has a kinky side.

Not many will admit it.

Some may not even know they have one,

Trust me,

You do.

We all do.

So, baby,

You act so good,

So above us.

You would never ever

Admit your kink exists.

But it does,

Come meet mine.

RESIST

Where are you, she wonders,

Lying across the bed.

She hears the lock slide.

Her body erupts with heat.

"Hey baby," she greets her lover.

He strips as he scurries towards her.

His arms draw her into his tall, firm body.

Their passion is beyond any fantasy she'd had of

him.

"I'm sorry for all of it," he whispers into her

delicate neck.

His flawless lips caressing her.

Her mouth slowly turned upward.

She knew he couldn't resist her.

DEVOUR

My sweet fantasy man,

How I devour you

In my dreams.

Your body amazes me,

Perfect in every way.

Boy Toy

Her boy toy.

A fun fuck.

She wanted him.

When she wanted him,

She'd text,

Give him a place and time.

She wanted a boy toy.

He was willing.

He was very able.

He satisfied her sexual needs.

He was her boy toy.

HEY, BABY

I'm drunk, baby.

Oh, how I want you.

How I long to touch you,

Suck you.

Feel you inside me.

Hey, baby,

I miss you.

How was it

When you touched me?

Held me?

Hey, baby,

I fucking want you.

you

I want to wrap my arms

Around you.

Crawl into you.

Devour all of you.

Kiss you.

Hold you.

Taste you.

Fuck you.

PLACES

The places I want you.

In your office.

On your desk.

Your car.

The beach.

The condo.

The bed.

The kitchen.

The shower.

The pool.

Anywhere.

Those are the places

I want you and

Many, many more...

PLEASE

Take me.

Penetrate me.

Fuck me,

Please.

Pound me.

Smack my body

With yours,

Please.

Taste me.

Lick me.

Suck me,

Please,

Baby,

Please.

I WANT

To fuck you senseless.

To make you scream my name.

To ride your steel rod all night long.

To mad fuck you.

Scream your name

While you pound my body.

I lay and take you in deep.

My body climaxes multiple times.

I pound your firm chest

As I ride to my bliss,

Your rod penetrating so far into me.

I fucking want you.

BEACH GRASS

Seeing the tall grass

As I relax on the beach.

Reminiscing of us laying together

Between the mounds

Of beach grass.

Making love so tender.

Feeling you inside me.

Your lips touching mine.

Threading my fingers through your brown hair.

The tall beach grass keeps us hidden

From those who don't understand

The draw between us.

The burning desire.

The risk.

THINGS

The things I want to do to you,

With you,

For you.

From sweet to naughty.

The list of things is long.

I'll let it all to your imagination.

SHAFT

His embrace,

While unexpected,

Was welcomed.

Holding him tight,

Drawing his body to her.

His arms bring her closer,

Their bodies forming one.

Another pass of his hand,

One last squeeze into him.

His body spoke to hers.

She smiles into his chest

When she feels his shaft.

Hard, long, wanting her.

A shared secret desire.

PEACH

She remembers the curve of his peach.

So soft, smooth, round.

Her hand squeezes his peach

With each orgasm he gave her.

Her fingers went bumpety-bump upon each

ripple.

She rode him to her bliss.

She remembers her rides fondly.

His ripples, and his peach

So perfect to caress.

One day she'll feel them again…

When truth sets him free.

TOUCH ME

Touch me with your eyes.

Look deep inside mine.

Touch me with your smile

When your lips meet mine.

Touch me with your mind.

Bring us together

With your thoughts.

Touch my body with your fingertips.

Draw along my curves.

Touch my body with your tongue.

Taste my sweet center.

Touch my body with your soul.

Meld us into one.

Touch my heart with your love.

Keep me safe.

Love me hard.

Touch my life with you.

Never leave me.

Never hurt me.

Touch me.

STRAP ME UP

One around each ankle.

Strap me up, baby.

One around each wrist

Strap me up, honey.

Pull them tight.

Hear me moan.

Fuck me hard.

Make me scream.

Strap me up, baby.

Oh, please,

Strap me up.

CAN'T WAIT

I can't wait to feel you between my thighs.

Your tongue licking my center walls.

Your hands tight upon my hips,

Holding me still as I squirm when I come.

I can't wait for your hard shaft to penetrate

Deep into me.

Thrust my body

Make me scream.

I can't wait to kiss you.

Hold you.

Fuck you.

Just once, baby.

Just once.

I can't wait.

DRAG

Drag your tongue across me.

From my mouth to my clit.

Taste me.

Make me tremble.

Drag your cock between my legs.

Thrust into me.

Push deep.

Make me scream.

Drag me baby.

All night long.

SEATED

You're seated in your chair across the room.

I sip on my cherry whiskey.

The TV is on.

I stand, walk towards you,

Sit on your lap.

I feel you rise beneath me.

We kiss.

Passions flair.

Your mouth finds my breasts.

My nipples harden as you make me wet.

Take me on the floor, baby.

Fuck me,

Now!

SWEET DREAMS

Sweet dreams of laying on the beach,

Watching the sunset, laying in your arms.

Your hand travels my body

Finding the curves, the silly spots,

The ecstasy spots.

Although, I am hot,

Chills cover me when your breath caresses

My shoulder.

Your lips move closer to mine.

The sun sets as you move us together.

Our bodies meld into one.

One day, dreams come true.

Sweet dreams baby.

Sweet dreams.

ONLY YOU

I would let you,

Only you,

Do things to me

No one else can.

Only you, baby.

Only you.

DRIZZLE

I wanna

Spray soft whipped cream,

Drizzle sweet chocolate syrup

Onto your body.

Top you off with a bright red cherry.

You are a delicious dessert.

Drizzle on me, baby.

I SALIVATE

When you appear in front of me,

I salivate.

I want to taste every inch of you.

My body becomes electric.

I am wet.

When you are the star of my dreams,

I tremble, quiver, and shake.

I want you.

I need you.

Take me.

I'm yours.

Every time I think of you,

And how delicious you are,

I salivate.

BANG

Make me go bang, baby.

Like a firecracker in the night sky.

Make my body explode in all directions.

Sending brilliant colors through my mind.

Make me scream your name out loud

As you go bang inside me.

Hold me.

Kiss me.

Make me go bang, baby.

Make me go bang.

I Fuck You

I fuck you

Every night

In my dreams.

Baby, you are

Magnificent.

I scream your name.

I ride you for hours.

You make me feel

Extraordinarily sensual.

Your mouth covers mine.

Your velvety tongue tastes me.

Your hands, oh my, your hands.

They are magical.

Touch me, baby.

In my dreams, you are the one I want.

RAVAGE ME

Take me.

Pound my body

All night long.

Ravage me.

Get rough with me.

I know you want to.

I saw that look in your eyes

When we were alone.

You want to ravage me.

That urge will haunt you.

One day you will

Ravage me.

FAN

Lying naked on the bed,

Her sweat drenched body

Being cooled by the ceiling fan.

The fan spins fast.

The air cool,

She closes her eyes.

Her vision of him walking towards her

Makes her body hot inside.

The ceiling fan spins round and round.

It wasn't cooling her,

Her fantasy's too hot.

Naked, ready for her,

He teases her,

Dragging himself against her.

Above her,

He grins mischievously,

Leaning down,

He captures her mouth.

She wakens from her daydream,

Her body glistening, aching,

Wanting her fantasy to be real.

PEERS

He peers up at her

From between her creamy thighs.

His gorgeous, naughty smile

Makes her weak.

She's ready to explode,

Moisten his face.

She gazes back at him,

Fists his soft brown hair,

Pushes his face

Into her heat,

And screams his name out loud.

PLEASE. DON'T. STOP.

Scintillating pleasures

Come over her

As he touches her,

Whisper kisses her lips,

Her body.

He glides his velvet tongue

Into her.

She quivers as he tastes her.

She moans in between,

Gasping for air.

"Please. Don't. Stop."

SLIP

Slip your hands around my waist.

Draw me in.

Embrace me tight.

Slip your tongue past my lips.

Taste me.

Slip your voice into my ear.

Tell me you want me.

Slip your body between my legs.

Penetrate me deep.

Make me moan.

Slip your love into my heart.

Promise to be mine.

And mine alone.

Slip it all into my life.

Make us one.

OLD FASHIONED

Old fashioned,

Moonshine cherries.

Kentucky bourbon.

Tennessee whiskey.

Sipping down that old fashioned,

Kentucky bourbon trailing down my throat.

One day, baby,

I hope that it's you

Instead of the bourbon.

LEMME

Lemme ride you.

Cover your mouth with mine.

Taste your deliciousness.

Lemme sit on you,

Bump my fingers along your tight body.

Caress your ripples.

Lemme feel you inside me,

Filling me with your heat.

Make me scream aloud.

Lemme ride you, love.

All night long.

All my life.

LICK ME, BABY

Lick me, baby.

I know you wanna.

I saw that look in your eyes

More than once.

It was there each time we met.

Your eyes gave you away

When they met mine.

I knew you wanted to

Lick me, baby.

FERRIS WHEEL

Riding on the Ferris Wheel as the fair closes.

Just us, no one else around.

I move to your side.

The bucket rocks.

You smile.

Knowing my plan,

I straddle your body,

Lower your shorts,

Slide onto your rod.

The Ferris Wheel goes round and round,

Seemingly, never ending.

We kiss.

We fuck.

I shout out your name when the wheel stops at the

top.

The bucket rocks as we hold on tight.

That Ferris Wheel ride…

Oh my…

ANYWHERE

Where do I want you?

Anywhere.

Everywhere.

Always.

Where would I fuck you?

Anywhere.

Everywhere.

Always.

Where would I wait for you?

Anywhere.

Everywhere.

Always.

TOUCH ME

Touch me here,

Touch me there,

With your mouth,

Then your hands.

Touch me, baby.

All over my body

With yours.

YOUR HANDS

Caress me with your hands.

Trace my curves with your fingers.

Cup my breasts.

Let your hands travel down my body.

Slip them between my thighs.

Tease me.

Slowly slither your fingers into me.

Feel my wetness.

It's all for you.

Let me crawl onto you.

Place myself unto your shaft.

Ride you for hours.

Squeal your name.

As your hands grasp my waist,

Pump my body with your thrusts.

I want to feel your heat

Throughout me.

With your hands,

Draw me close.

Press your lips to mine.

Devour me.

MY BODY

I want you to kiss

My body.

Begin with my lips,

And taste me.

I want you to kiss

My body.

Down my neck;

My shoulder.

Suck on my nipples.

Tease me.

I want you to kiss

My body.

Follow my curves down,

Down to my center.

Place your lips on my inner thigh.

Let your tongue find its way

Into me.

Take me baby.

My body.

My soul.

My all.

YOUR BODY

I want to begin to kiss

Your body.

At your ankle,

Up your calf.

Kiss your knee,

Then your thigh.

When I reach that part of

Your body,

Your center,

I want to take you in my mouth.

Pleasure you

Until you tremble beneath me.

Until your body quivers, shakes and throbs

As I swallow all of you.

I want to kiss

Your body

Over your rippled abs,

Your rib cage,

Your pecs,

Your shoulder to

Your neck.

I want to kiss

Your body

All the way from your ankle to your lips.

Devour your body,

Your mind, and soul.

Taste your essence.

Breathe you into me.

I want

Your body.

I want you.

MAD FUCK

She wants to mad fuck him.

Strap him down.

Climb onto him.

Ride his stiff cock

For hours

Until

It's limp.

She wants him to mad fuck her.

Pound her body,

Hard,

With such a force

She screams his name.

She claws his back.

She wants him like no other.

SMOTHER

I want to smother you in my cleavage.

Feel your soft hair tickling my breasts.

Smother you with my wet pussy

As your silky hair wisps my thighs.

Your tongue sends me to ecstasy.

Then your body smothers me in love.

Fill me with your hard shaft.

Smother my slick tunnel with your cum.

Take me.

Fuck me.

All night long.

PICK ME

Pick me, baby.

Place your soft hands around my waist.

Pick me up,

Embrace my body with your smooth arms.

Fist my long blonde hair.

Kiss me hard.

I wrap my legs around you,

Thread my fingers through your brown hair.

I taste you with my tongue.

My body opens for you.

You enter me.

Our passion is fierce.

C'mon, baby.

Pick me.

SUIT

I envision you in a suit.

Standing there so beautiful.

Nothing out of place.

I want to touch you,

Thread my fingers with yours,

And walk together

Into the sunset.

My God, my heart races,

My breathing rapid.

My body quivers

As my vision of you in that suit

Becomes so clear.

So real.

COME

Your fingertips glide along my curves,

Tracing my hips,

Slipping between my soft thighs

Into my wet folds.

I sigh into your warm mouth,

Kissing me deeply.

Passionately.

Sliding your body down, down,

Your silky hair brushes my inner thigh.

I quiver and moan.

Your velvety tongue slides inside me.

I come as you enjoy every drop.

Your body envelops mine,

Our lust binding us as one.

OH MY

The feel of my fingertips bumping across your

abs,

Finding my treasure with my lips.

Oh my.

To taste your sweetness

Sliding down my throat.

How I long for this deep within me.

Oh my.

DREAM

I dream of that day,

Finally

Alone with you.

Gazing deep into your soul.

I dream of your hands caressing

My bare skin.

I dream of your soft hair

Tickling me.

I dream of your tongue

Licking me.

I dream of wrapping my body

Around yours.

I dream of embracing you again,

Holding you close to me again.

Feeling, sensing, knowing you dream it, too.

TAKE ME

Take me.

Make me scream.

Give me chills.

Make me quiver.

Take me.

Make me wet.

Make my heart race.

Make me sweat.

Take me.

You know you want to.

Come to me, baby.

Take me!

CLIMB

Slowly, she climbs his six-foot four body.

Kissing his creamy soft skin,

His rippled abs,

His firm pecs.

Her lips glide across him.

His body glistens as his cock hardens beneath her.

She climbs her lover.

He licks his lips.

She captures his tongue with her mouth on his.

So damn delicious.

His penetration is forceful.

Deep into her wet, hot pussy.

They embrace,

Holding on so tightly

As they become one.

TABLE

He scoops her up,

Carries her to the table.

Biting her lip,

She blinks slowly.

He finds that sweet spot on her neck.

She sighs.

Her body shivers when his lips graze her skin.

Arching her back,

She invites him in.

"Please, baby," she moans.

He slithers his long fingers between her soft

thighs.

Reaching behind her,

Sliding her ass to the edge of the table,

He thrusts his hot cock into her.

Their bodies becoming one,

Making beautiful love

On the table.

SHOWER

Eyes closed,

Water cascading down her petite body.

Cool air brushes her.

Her lips curve upward.

His arms embrace her, drawing her in.

She melts into his tall, lean body.

His lips softly touch her left shoulder.

His tongue traces the frame of her face.

Finding her mouth,

They kiss.

Hot passionate, deep, unending kisses.

He lifts her.

He enters her.

He loves her.

COOKIE JAR

He wanted to dip into her cookie jar.

He knows he did.

He saw that same look in her eyes.

He sent her those vibes.

Telling her

He wanted that cookie from her cookie jar.

She'll be ready when he comes back.

She knows he wants to.

That cookie in her cookie jar

Will always be there for him to take.

Timing is everything.

Now isn't the time.

She's patient.

She'll bide her time.

She says to him in her dreams,

"So, baby, when you're ready,

Come find my cookie jar.

The lid is loose.

Open it, reach in.

Take that cookie.

You know you want to."

BETWEEN

Lying on the sofa,

Clothes crumbled on the floor,

They lay skin to skin.

His hand travels between her breasts.

Teasing her, she quivers.

Her body is hot

As his hand reaches between her thighs.

He's made it to her center.

She sighs.

She moans.

His fingers slip into her folds,

Feeling her heat.

His lips are soft against her neck.

He breathes into her ear,

"Baby, I want you; I want you now."

Her lips curve upward as she knows

He's hers.

She has him under her spell.

NAKED

I want you naked

In my bed,

Against the wall,

In the shower,

On any surface,

Anywhere, anytime.

I want you naked

With me.

I WANT YOU

Like a baby wants to be held,

A morning person wants coffee,

I want you.

Like dancers want to dance,

And singers want to sing,

I want you.

Like writers want to write,

And lovers want to love,

I want you.

Like kids want candy

On Halloween night,

I want you.

DON'T LET ME ESCAPE

I want you between my warm thighs,

Your soft curls tickling me.

Kiss my inner thighs with your full lips.

Slide one finger into my hot core

And another as you thumb my clit.

Make my body quiver when your tongue slithers

along my folds.

Taste me, love.

Hold me down.

Make me scream.

Don't let me escape.

Make me come like never before.

Fuck me until I can't move.

HONEY

Honey,

I want you.

Everywhere.

Anytime.

Anyplace.

All the time.

Honey,

Come take me.

Kiss me.

Hold me.

Touch me.

Taste me.

Finger me.

Fuck me until I can't breathe.

Honey, please.

FUCK RUG

You're holding me tenderly,

Caressing me softly.

Your full lips

Tastes my skin,

Giving me chills.

The fireplace's heat warms me

As we lay on our fuck rug.

Your body next to mine,

Your eyes gazing deeply into my soul.

Whispering, "I love you,"

Reminding me of where I belong.

My heart is filled with love for you,

Always only you.

Making love on our fuck rug.

Soft, furry, plush.

Our fuck rug.

The fibers tickle me.

Your tongue arouses me.

Your love protects me.

FAVORITE TOY

It wasn't her vibrator,

Or her dildo.

No.

Her favorite toy

Was, and always will be, him.

She knew when and where he worked.

She made sure to request his presence when he

was available.

Without fail,

He'd come to her.

And be her favorite toy.

I WANTED TO

I wanted to

Clear the room.

Lock the door.

Pull off your mask.

Yank off your white coat.

Tear off your green scrubs.

I wanted to

Rip off my clothes.

Climb onto the exam room table

And kiss your lips.

Slide my tongue into your warm mouth,

Caress your tall, tight body.

Dig my nails into your shoulder blades.

Leave my mark on your sweet, pale skin.

I wanted you

To make me scream your name

As you fucked me senseless.

Pounding my body

With yours.

I wanted to have you

Just as you did me.

PLAYER

You know you wanted her.

The way you looked at her,

Smiled at her,

Touched her,

Held her.

You're a player,

Buy ya got caught.

Your balls got snipped.

Tossed her under the bus

To protect your ass.

When ya get those balls back,

Player,

She'll be ready.

Stop fighting that urge.

She knows you want her.

WHISKEY NIGHT

It's so good spilling down my throat.

My thoughts wonder to you.

How are you, baby?

Whiskey night brings me closer to you.

I know you enjoy it.

Just like me.

Let's share a whiskey night, baby.

Let our inhibitions run free.

Tie me up,

Fuck me hard.

Make me scream

All night long.

One time, baby.

It's all I want.

You, me, whiskey night.

When you're ready,

I know you want it.

You always will.

So, find me, baby.

Satisfy that urge.

FORBIDDEN

Forbidden to one another.

Once their souls met,

All bets were off.

Lines erased.

Rules broken.

To the outside world

They pretended,

Misleading those around them.

Tricking, lying, sneaking out.

Secret rendezvous.

The forbidden desire they shared.

Wanting to touch.

Needing to hold.

Press their bodies together

And release their forbidden passions.

LET'S PLAY

Now that you've convinced everyone

You're without flaws,

Would never play outside the box,

Always follows the rules,

Never cross the line,

Come find me, love.

Let's play around.

Be risky,

Daring, and bold.

Break the rules.

Have some fun.

Let's play.

MAYBE, BABY

Maybe, baby,

I read your mind.

Knew your sinful thoughts.

But,

Maybe, baby,

You got caught

Wanting me.

And

Maybe, baby,

You can have

What you want.

Just

Take that chance, play that game.

Break those rules.

Cross that line.

MOAN

The sound of you letting out a soft moan as I

make my way down.

Kissing your chest,

My lips take a ride across those abs.

Almost to your treasure.

Another delicious moan escapes your body

Making me seep between my folds.

Your fingers fist my long hair, winding it around

your hand.

My tongue teases you around your tip,

Drawing your body into bliss,

Causing another deep, louder moan from the

depths of your soul.

My mouth engulfs you,

Sucking long and hard.

Feeling you throb, knowing you're close,

I move faster upon your shaft.

One last moan escapes from you.

Oh, baby,

You taste so sweet.

WE WANT

We want the same.

You want me.

I want you.

All day, every day.

All night, every night.

We want the same.

Hold me in your arms.

Press your lips to mine.

Lay between my legs.

Taste me with your tongue.

We want the same.

To love, and like.

Be true, and honest.

Fun and exciting.

Romantic and beautiful.

Dream about me, baby.

Cause we want the same.

SOFT

I love your soft skin touching mine.

Your soft hands upon my body.

Your soft lips kissing me.

Your soft face between my thighs.

Your soft hair tickling me.

Your soft tongue

Licks me,

Tastes me,

Devours me.

All night long, baby.

JUST ONCE

Just once

Was what she wanted.

What she convinced herself

Was all it was.

Just one time with him,

She swore,

To hold him,

Kiss him,

Fuck him,

Just once.

FANTASY

You became my fantasy.

Hot, delicious, fabulous fantasy.

My dreams were so vivid.

My body shook in the dark of the night.

Though just a dream,

Your lips softly pressed with mine.

Our fingers locked as you entered me.

Only in my fantasy did this occur.

You were, you are, and you will always be

My beautiful fantasy.

My muse.

HOT

He was so damn hot.

So, fucking hot!

He drove her crazy

When he came into her dreams.

She wanted him.

Time passed.

Her desires grew.

She played with him in her fantasies.

He was so perfect there.

He made he feel special.

He made her ache for him.

His eyes scorched her soul.

Despite everything,

He's still so damn hot!

LOVER

Hey, lover.

I miss your touch.

I need your touch.

I miss your kiss.

I need your kiss.

I miss our bond.

I need our bond.

Please come back to me,

Lover.

I miss us.

I need us.

I miss you.

I need you.

I love you.

LAST NIGHT

I dreamt about you last night.

We made love for hours.

Your fingers traveled across my breasts,

Down my ribcage,

Passed my navel,

And into my folds.

Your tongue explored every crevasse of my body.

You held me tenderly in your arms,

Kissing me passionately.

My lips glided over your firm chest,

Down your abs

To your hardness.

You tasted delicious in my dreams.

My body melded into yours when you penetrated

me.

My dream was perfect.

Last night,

It was us.

HE

He wants her.

He can't admit it.

Not yet.

But he knows.

He wants her.

SORRY, NOT SORRY

Sorry, not sorry.

You are my forever fantasy.

You cannot stop my dreams,

Or my desire for you.

You are the one I want.

Sorry, not sorry,

For being attracted to you.

Your beautiful smile,

Your fuck me eyes.

Your body spoke to mine,

And your touch melted me.

So sorry, not sorry.

WANT

I want to fuck you.

Taste you.

Take you into me.

I've wanted to for a while.

I won't deny it.

I want you.

Forever.

I want you.

AFTER MIDNIGHT HOURS

As I lie in my bed

After midnight hours,

A gorgeous vision

Appears in my dreams.

He is perfect as his lips touch mine.

His body slowly melds into me.

He enters me.

We make love

After midnight hours.

DROP-DEAD GORGEOUS

He was drop-dead gorgeous.

Every inch of his six-foot-four body.

Drop-dead gorgeous.

His dark brown hair was perfectly combed,

Not one luscious strand out of place.

His blue eyes were pools she wanted to swim in

forever.

Those glasses.

There was something about those damn glasses,

though.

She wished for his strong arms to embrace her as

he had before.

For his big, soft hands to swallow hers as they did

at one time.

His long fingers tantalizing her senses as they

softly touch her skin when they were close.

He was drop-dead gorgeous.

DREAMS

I can't have you in real life.

I can have you in my dreams.

And in my dreams,

I do.

You are perfect

In my dreams.

The way you caress me,

Your lips on mine,

Your hands touching me,

Your blue eyes piercing my soul.

I thread my fingers through your dark brown hair.

I trace your smooth jawline with my palm.

In my dreams,

You are everything I want,

Everything I desire, crave, wish for.

Maybe one day,

My dreams will come true.

DRINK

You took it home.

You poured yourself a drink,

A drink of the bourbon.

You read it.

Maybe the card again.

You liked them all

Because they were hot.

You got off on them,

But you got caught.

Have another drink, baby.

Think of me

When you do.

I go down

Just as easy.

Just as smooth.

PEEK

Did you get a peek?

During surgery?

When my gown moved

From my shoulder,

Did it slip too far?

Did you get a peek?

Is that when

You cast your spell?

Whispered in my ear?

Brushed your hand

Against my breast?

Was it just a peek?

MINE

You were never mine

In real life.

I made you mine

In my dreams.

ME

One day, you'll miss me.

Come fine me, baby.

I'll be here

When you realize

You miss me.

You'll wonder about me,

About what could've been.

How I would feel in your arms.

The smell of my skin.

The taste of me when we kiss.

Call me, baby.

You'll find your answers.

They lie

Within

Me.

DESIRE

Her desire for him is as strong as it ever was.

After all that has transpired,

She still desires his touch,

His body, his all.

Her feelings have changed.

The love has waned.

Yet, her desire to be with him has strengthened.

She feels him when she closes her eyes.

She knows he feels the same.

When he dreams,

She goes to him.

They are together in each other's dreams.

KISS ME, BABY

You know you wanted to.

As much as I wanted you to.

That last meeting alone,

In that small room…

Had I removed your mask,

Leaned in,

You would've kissed me.

I saw it in your eyes.

The closeness of how you sat to me.

Your soft tone.

Your arms holding me.

Kiss me, baby.

I know you want to.

NAUGHTY

He's inside you.

I've seen him.

Through your gorgeous eyes,

He gazed into my soul.

I've felt him when your arm was around me that

first time,

Then your warm embrace.

My naughty creature inside me

Connected to yours.

He wanted to come out and play,

But you suppressed him.

You have appearances to uphold.

No worries, baby.

When your naughty creature is allowed,

Come find mine.

FUCK ME, BABY

I don't care what anyone says.

I want you.

I want you so damn much.

I ache for you to

Fuck me, baby.

No matter what happens,

I'll always want you.

Lie all you want.

You want me.

I know you do.

Come find me,

And fuck me, baby.

HANDS

I want to put my hands on you again.

Just like I did that time.

To hold you again

Against my body.

To feel your hands on me again.

Just like you did before

When you held me close.

I want to feel my hand in yours again.

Your hand engulfed mine.

Your hand was so soft, so gentle.

I want to feel your hands on me.

Just like before.

You know,

When we were alone

Together.

YES, I WOULD

I'd wrap myself around you in a fucking heartbeat.

A nanosecond, baby.

Crawl onto you.

Be trapped under you.

Yes, I would.

Before your eyes blinked or

Your breath was taken.

Ride you like no one ever has.

Make you scream my name, lover.

Yes, I would.

Oh, how I want to taste you.

Come, let's play,

Darlin'.

YOUR TOUCH

Your touch sent me to oblivion

When you touched my shoulder,

When your hand swallowed mine,

When your arm rested across my back,

When you embraced me completely.

Your touch melted my insides.

My body was electrified by

Your touch.

NEXT TO ME

I want to

Wake up

With you

Next to me.

Smiling at me

Lying naked

Next to me.

I want you

All the time.

I WANT YOU STILL

Like fish need water,

The sun has to shine.

Like the moon moves the tides,

I want you still.

Like flowers bloom,

Grass grows,

Bees pollinate,

I want you still.

Like kids want cake,

Like humans need air,

Like nymphomaniacs crave sex,

I want you still.

FOR YOU

When you realize I was right,

I'll be ready for you.

To hold me,

Kiss me,

Take me.

I'll wait forever

For you.

You're worth it.

I know you are.

I'm ready now,

Next week,

Next month,

Next year.

Whenever you're ready,

I'll hold you,

Kiss you,

Love you.

I'll wait forever

For you.

SPARK

You lit a spark inside me.

Each time I saw you,

The fire inside me grew.

That spark lit a flame

That would not die.

It blazed hotter every day.

After all that has transpired

Between us,

That spark,

That fire,

It's still burning for you

As hot as it ever was.

PLAY

Come play with me.

Meet me in secret.

Hide away with me.

Play with my body

Like I know you want to.

I saw that look in your eyes.

That mischievous twinkle when we were alone

together.

I heard it in your soft tone when you spoke with

me.

Asking how I was,

Your voice was almost a whisper

Against my cheek.

Play with me, baby,

Kiss me

Like you want to.

I've known for months you do.

When you held me,

That's when I knew for sure,

C'mon honey,

Let's play.

PURE

He acted so pure,

So, without fault.

His underlying naughty boy

Shone through when they were together.

His pure, clean, perfect facade

All fake.

The risk taker,

The wondering eyes,

Loose hands,

Mischievous smile.

That was the real man.

The devilish lover she enjoyed.

GLASSES

There's something about a man and glasses.

It's the Clark Kent/Superman syndrome.

Give me the glasses, baby.

I'll take Clark Kent over Superman any day.

Those glasses make you so fucking hot.

So mouthwateringly irresistible.

So, OMG delicious.

Wear those glasses when you kiss me,

When you undress me,

When you take me to bed.

Those damn glasses, baby.

FUN

It was fun

To flirt with you.

You enjoyed every second of it.

It was fun

Being alone with you.

It was fun

Holding you.

Feeling your body against mine.

It was so damn much

Fun!

HEY, BABY

Hey, baby,

Come find me.

You want it.

You know it.

Hey, baby,

I'm here.

Wanting you.

Like I know you want me too.

Hey, baby,

Don't be shy.

You can't fool me.

I know that vibe.

That look you gave me.

Hey, baby,

Call, text, email.

Whatever.

I know you wanna.

Hey, baby.

HOT IN HERE

It gets hot in here.

Be careful, baby.

Have that bourbon ready

When you read my work.

Better make it on the rocks

To help cool you down.

Which are your favorites?

Do you follow me?

Or just troll my pages?

Check up on me

Cause you just can't let go?

You're too curious, or

Are you waiting for a message?

It'll get hotter in here

In the days, weeks, months to come.

So, buckle up buttercup,

And enjoy the ride.

144

ALWAYS & FOREVER

No matter what,

I'll want you

Always and forever.

Hate me,

Love me,

No matter what.

I'll want you

Always and forever.

HER SCENT

She always wore the same perfume when she saw

him.

It seemed to perk him up more each time they

met.

She noticed little things about his behavior,

About his body.

His eyes smiled more.

They traveled her body.

His touch was gentler.

He sat closer to her.

Well within her personal space.

He was close enough to kiss.

She wanted to

But never did.

She respected him.

She was grateful to him,

She felt connected to him.

Her heart grew to love him.

Her body wanted him.

He told her the same

When he held her

That very last day.

YOUR EYES

Your eyes captured me.

The way you gazed into mine,

So deep,

So long.

I was hooked.

I want to swim into your eyes,

Drown within your soul.

Come take me, baby.

Take me all the way in.

BUZZED

When I'm buzzed,

I think of you.

What I want to do with you.

What you will do to me.

When I'm buzzed,

I want you so damn much, I ache.

I want to do things to you.

To make you moan.

When I'm buzzed,

I dream of your body

On me,

Fucking me.

When I'm buzzed,

You could have your way with me.

Whatever you want to do.

Hold me, kiss me, love me.

When I'm buzzed,

You are my favorite fantasy.

My dreams are wildly beautiful.

You and me, baby.

You and me!

MAYBE

He led her on,

Made her think...

Maybe.

His smile,

His eyes,

His body,

His touch,

His charm.

Everything

About him

Said

Maybe.

HE WANTS YOU

You've known it for a while.

That's why you did what you did.

He wants you.

For all those months,

He breathed you in.

He watched you closely.

He enjoyed your every move.

There was never a "no"

Because he wants you.

He lied to tell you.

Give him time.

He'll be back,

Because

He wants you.

SO DAMN HOT

She enjoyed her view,

Standing by the side,

Waiting on someone to pick her up.

Tall, fit, so damn hot.

She watched as he was greeted by his co-workers.

His smile as beautiful as she remembered.

He slung his bag over his shoulder,

Grabbed his food and soda before heading in.

He was still

So damn hot.

THANK YOU

To my incredibly loving and supportive husband.

I love you, always only you.

ABOUT THE AUTHOR

EB lives in Florida with her husband.

2020-21 was when EB found her voice through

pain and perseverance.

She put it all into words to share with the world.

Writing poetry is a release for her.

A form of therapy and self-healing.

www.ingramcontent.com/pod-product-compliance
Lightning Source LLC
Chambersburg PA
CBHW022057050726
47591CB00002B/576